Temptation

Edited by David Larkin

Temptation

Introduction by Virgil Pomfret

Picture Research by Celestine Dars

Pan Books Ltd.
London and Sydney

We are most grateful to the galleries, private collectors
and museums who have kindly allowed the use of material
in their copyright.

TEMPTATION

This edition published 1975 by Pan Books Limited
18-21 Cavaye Place, London SW10 9PG

ISBN 0 330 24608 9

PRINTED IN ITALY BY MONDADORI, VERONA

The only way to get rid of temptation is to yield to it.

OSCAR WILDE (1854-1900)

'You oughtn't to yield to temptation.'
'Well, somebody must, or the thing becomes absurd.'
SIR ANTHONY HOPE HAWKINS (1863-1933)

Temptation has been a subject central to the work of the artist throughout the ages. Whether or not one accepts the Old Testament story of man choosing knowledge by eating the forbidden fruit, it is fact that he has had an awareness of good and evil since the beginning of time. Temptation is inseparable from awareness and, as such, is a part of man's everyday life. The heightened response of the creative artist to human emotion and weakness has logically drawn him to the subject. It is a subject through which an important aspect of the history of painting can be traced, and one which painters have used to leave lasting social comment on the attitudes of their time.

We live in an age in which we are constantly bombarded with ephemeral images. It is a fundamentally

different age to any before it. With
its instant-influence machinery of
television and newspapers, it is a
commerce-dictated age for a so-called
permissive society. The advertising world is
self-congratulatory about the success of its
imagery in tempting the masses, believing that
it has originated excitingly new space-age
visual concepts without which the temptation
to buy would not exist. In reality the
symbolism is old, almost as old as art itself. It
is successful because it is obvious; but because
it is obvious, it is also ephemeral.

Despite the mass media, the paintings in this
book may make us wonder whether our age is
in fact more permissive than any other. They
are neither obvious nor ephemeral. Most of

the pictures have weathered the passage of
time and remain as fine and enigmatic as when
they were first conceived. The carefully
selected modern images only impart their
secrets to the imaginative or conscientious
observer. There is no transitory sensationalism
here and, although much of the symbolism is
the same, a huge gulf separates these paintings
from the instant pleasure giving creations of
today's media men.

This book does not, however, ignore the
contemporary artist's view of those advertising
agency exploited temptations. The three pieces
that together form Jacques Brissot's *The Hay
Wain* represent a remarkably complete
evocation of the media-governed temptations
of our time, and of us, the people who have

yielded to them. Freud, all-knowingly from his cloud of flowers, seems to be saying 'I told you so' and 'Now get yourselves out of that mess . . .' But temptation is ageless, and if Brissot convinces us for a moment that we live in the generation that first surrendered to it, most of the earlier paintings will quickly dispel that impression.

Nearly five centuries seperate *The Hay Wain* from *The Last Judgement* of Hieronimus Bosch, and it may be that all they have in common is their multiplicity of images. But if we believe the theories of Wilhelm Franger on Bosch and the motivation behind his paintings, then Bosch was a member of a sect that was amazingly permissive even by today's standards. The sect, The Brothers and Sisters of the Free Spirit or Adamites, believed that Adam, as the first man on earth, was the true God. They ate freely from the tree of temptation in all its guises and indulged in sexual perversion as a religious ritual. Franger believed that the symbolism in Bosch's paintings was a coherent representation of the beliefs of this heretical sect.

Breughel the Elder's view of temptation was very different. But in his painting *The Triumph of Death* he did little to champion the cause of those fighting it. His forces of good—those people avoiding all forms of temptation—however strong, will always be defeated by the army of death. He gives the impression that there is no reward on this earth for those delivered from temptation and evil.

The words of George Bernard Shaw, 'You use a glass mirror to see your face: you use works of art to see your soul,' seem very appropriate to the paintings in this book. It would not be possible for one person to give a definitive account of what was in the minds of the artists when they painted them; nor would one person's interpretations be likely to agree with those of even a small group of other observers. It is an essential part of viewing such a collection of pictures that the individual, consciously or unconsciously, puts his experience of life and personality into finding a satisfactory explanation for himself. Some people will wonder what is particularly relevant to temptation in several of the pictures chosen; others will find that the same pictures come closest to being a mirror of their own temptations.

If Balthus' *La Chambre* seems an appropriate work to discuss in the context of Shaw's words, it is for reasons other than that the girl is looking at her face in a mirror. What is behind that enigmatic face? Is she just a narcissist taking pleasure in her own beauty? Or is she imagining the pleasures that she will demand of her anonymous lover? However you interpret this lovely painting, beware: It is bound to reflect something of your soul.

Unlike the paintings already discussed, the apparent simplicity of the Balthus picture accounts for much of its success. He has created enigma through pose, facial expression and the anonymity of the male character. How different an effect this picture would have if Balthus had failed with these subtle elements. Four centuries earlier Lucas Cranach used two of these elements in his painting *The Mismatched Couple*. It is only through their expressions and poses that we are able to recognize the relationship between the rich merchant and the much younger beautiful girl. They may seem strange bedfellows, but satisfied lust on the one hand and acquisition of wealth on the other seem to be adequate compensations. There can be no doubt that they will stay together longer than the lovers in Gervex's *Rolla*.

By way of contrast a number of paintings have been chosen that are more easily understood by knowing the symbolism employed. Certain symbols, particularly in this context those representing good and evil and those with sexual connotations, have been developed by artists over many centuries.

These have been used not only to veil the obvious, but also to circumvent the laws banning certain aspects of overt representation as obscene or offensive.

Simple symbols, such as the devil representing evil and winged angels for good, have made way for more complex images: snakes, erect columns and even trees, either exaggerated or used apparently out of context, represent the phallus. It is quite logical that the artist eventually reached a point where an entire painting becomes a symbol in itself. Among the paintings of this kind, *Extasé* by Koch and Suzy Gablick's *Simulations* are fascinating examples. At first glance, Koch's painting is of a curiously barren garden inhabited only by a scantily clad girl listening to an old gramophone. What can this mean? In its separate parts, probably nothing; but, seen as a whole, the scene takes on significance. The entrance to the garden at the bottom surely represents the vagina leading to the womb. If *Simulations* is open to a similar translation, then it is only the fertile appearance of the sun compared to the barren feeling of the Koch painting that contrasts them.

Temptation, in all its different guises, is the catalyst in the fight between good and evil. Van Eyck recognizes this fact in *The Last Judgement*. He sees our response to it as deciding our fate in the after-life. His painting quite simply states that if we yield to temptation we go to Hell; if we resist, our reward is a place in Heaven. He makes no suggestion that there are different degrees of yielding to temptation: Lust, violence and

self-righteousness are equal evils.

The paintings have been selected to show a wide variety of temptations in many different styles, from deeply religious works to the most overtly sexual. If Dali attempts to outrage us by depicting chastity as an odious form of self-righteousness, he is no more likely to offend us than Romano, whose use of fantasy elements, over 400 years earlier, does nothing to veil the overt realism of the voyeur watching an act of rape. If Memling's *St John*, with its religious imagery, is a refreshing contrast, there is still no doubt that for a moment the evangelist is himself guilty of the sins of self-satisfaction and glory seeking.

It is possible to disagree with these interpretations; indeed they should be ignored if other impressions seem more satisfying or appropriate. Levy Dhurmer's *Silence* amply demonstrates how widely varied people's views of these paintings can be. As the final painting in the book, it can be seen as the question mark at the end of a sentence. There can be no definitive interpretation: its success lies in the thousand meanings that can be attributed to it. Indeed every picture has been chosen with one aim in mind—to arouse a wide range of responses from the observer. The veiled suggestion of temptation in the religious pictures, the extremes of passion realized in the mythological and fantasy subjects, the luxurious indulgences of the Pre-Raphaelites, and the modern exaggerated ideals of temptation like Bellmer's *Small Painting of a Doll* are all as likely to achieve that aim as those discussed in greater detail.

The more you look, the greater will be the rewards. Fine paintings offer few of their secrets to the casual viewer. If you find yourself transported into a world of fantasy or, like Shaw, see a mirror-image of your soul, then the artist has succeeded in one of his aims—he has elicited a response.

VIRGIL POMFRET

There are several good protections against temptation, but the surest is cowardice.

MARK TWAIN (1835-1910)

1) The Last Judgement

22¼ x 7¾"

JAN VAN EYCK

1422-1441

Fletcher Fund 1933,
Metropolitan Museum of Art, New York

2) Detail from The Last Judgement
HIERONIMUS BOSCH
1452-1516
Akademie der Bilden Künste, Vienna

3) Detail from The Last Judgement
HIERONIMUS BOSCH
1452-1516

Akademie der Bilden Künste, Vienna

4) Detail from The Last Judgement

HIERONIMUS BOSCH

1452-1516

Akademie der Bilden Künste, Vienna

5) Detail from The Garden of Delights

1973   61 ½ x 122 ½"

JACQUES BRISSOT

Galerie Kerchache, Paris

6) The Hay Wain (Left Panel of Triptych)
1973   80 x 72"
JACQUES BRISSOT

Galerie Kerchache, Paris

7) The Hay Wain (Center Panel of Triptych)
1973   80 x 72"
JACQUES BRISSOT

Galerie Kerchache, Paris

8) The Hay Wain (Right Panel of Triptych)
1973   80 x 72"
JAQUES BRISSOT
Galerie Kerchache, Paris

9) The Mismatched Couple
1553
LUCAS CRANACH
1472-1553
Nuremberg Museum
Photo—Giraudon

10) Triumph of Death
BRUEGHEL the Elder
c. 1525-1569

Prado Museum, Madrid
Photo—Faillet/Ziolo

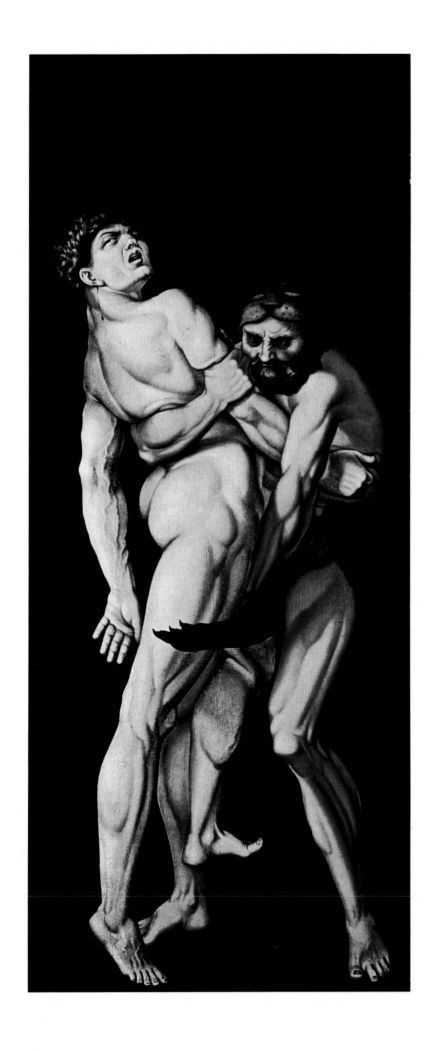

11) Hercule and Antée
1530
HANS BALDUNG GRIEN
1484-1545

Cassel Museum
Photo—Giraudon

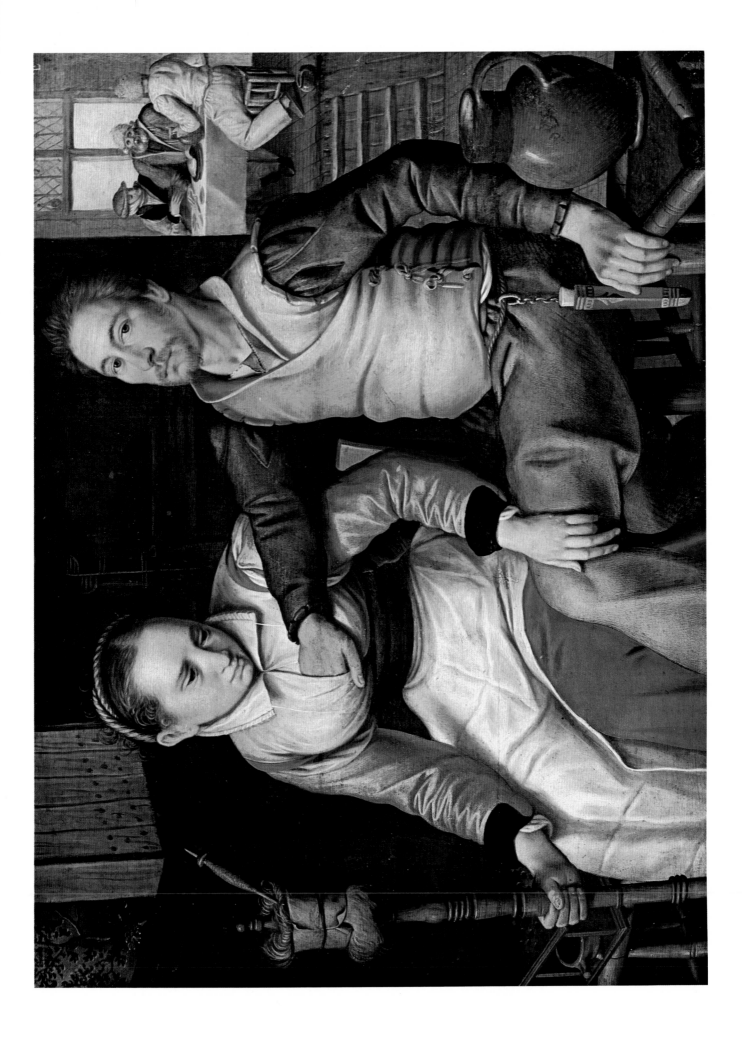

12) The Country Lovers
PETER AERTSEN
1508-1575

Kunsthistorischesmuseum, Vienna
Photo—Meyer

13) Fragment Study for The Last Judgement
HIERONIMUS BOSCH
1452-1516

Alte Pinakothek, Munich
Photo—Blauel

14) Mythological Erotic Scene
GIULIO ROMANO
c. 1495-1546
Palazzo del Té, Mantova
Photo—Scala

15) Jesus denied as a King
FRA ANGELICO
c. 1387-1455

Museo San Marco, Florence
Photo—Scala

16) St. John the Evangelist at Patmos
(Right Panel of Triptych)
HANS MEMLING
c. 1430-1494

Memling Museum, Bruges
Photo—Scala

17) Crucifixion
1958
STANLEY SPENCER
1891-1959

Aldenham School, Elstree
Photo—M. Slingsby

18) Satan, Sin and Death

c. 1735   24⅜ x 29⅜″

WILLIAM HOGARTH

1697-1764

Tate Gallery, London

Photo—M. Slingsby

112 Phillip Problems. Study-Sketch by Richard Buhr. Died 18th 1907. Bethlehem Hospital, London. St. George's in the Fields.

19) The Child's Problem
1857   6¾ x 10"
RICHARD DADD
1817-1886

Tate Gallery, London
Photo—M. Slingsby

20) Brunhilde and Gunther
HENRY FUSELI
1741-1825
Nottingham Museum

21) Ferdinand lured by Ariel
1849   25½ x 20″
JOHN EVERETT MILLAIS
1829-1896

The Makins Collection
Photo—M. Holford

22) Antony and Cleopatra
1883   25¾ x 36½"
LAWRENCE ALMA-TADEMA
1836-1912
Courtesy of Sotheby's, London

23) The Roses of Heliogabalus
1888   52 x 84⅛"
LAWRENCE ALMA-TADEMA
1836-1912

Courtesy of Sotheby's, London

24) Vain Courtship

1900   30½ x 16¼″

LAWRENCE ALMA-TADEMA

1836-1912

Courtesy of Sotheby's, London

25) Simulations
1970   8 x 10″
SUZY GABLICK
The Artist's Collection

26) Spleen and Ideal
1896
CARLOS SCHWAB
Collection G. Lévy, Paris
Photo—Snark

27) Flotsam
1873
JULES GARNIER

Dijon Museum
Photo—Bulloz

28) Pornokrates
1896   27¾ x 18″
FERDINAND ROPS

M. Mabille Collection, Brussels
Photo—ACL

29) Rolla
1878
HENRI GERVEX
1852-1929

Bordeaux Museum
Photo—Bulloz

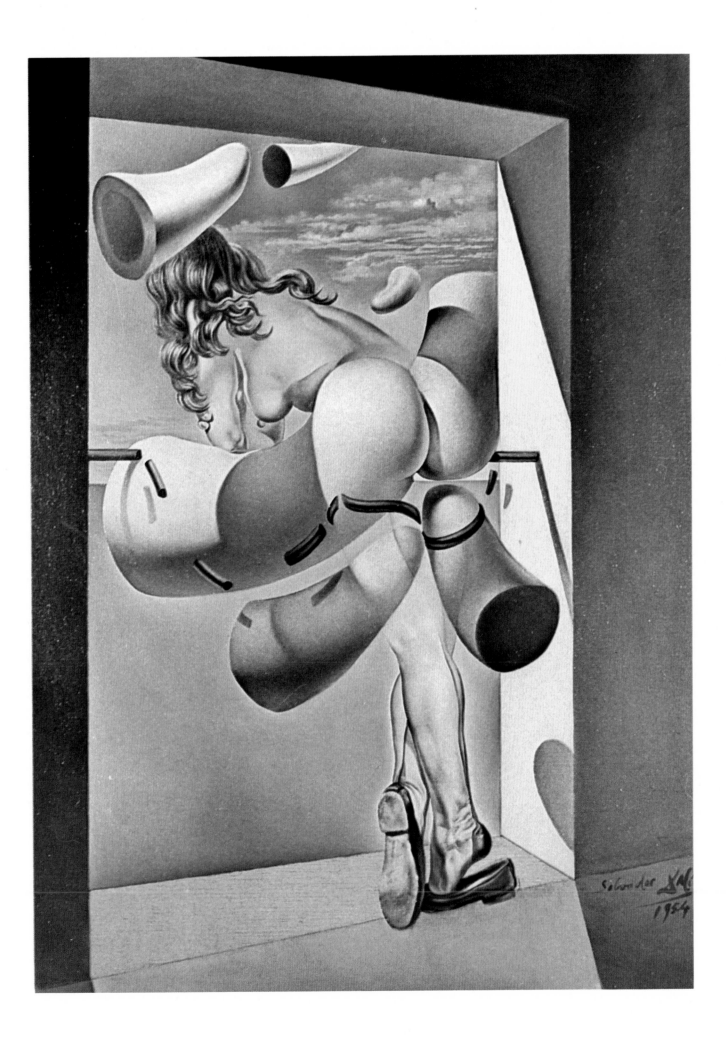

30) Young Virgin auto-sodomized by her own chastity

1954

SALVADOR DALI

Playboy Collection, USA

31) Woman Reclining
c. 1925
DOMINIQUE PEYRONNET

Museum of Modern Art, Paris
Photo—Held/Ziolo

32) Maternal Instinct
1972
JAMES LLOYD
Portal Gallery, London
Photo—M. Slingsby

33) The Two Hemispheres
1967-69
ERNST FUCHS
1930-
Collection of F. Grohe, Germany

34) The Widow

1969   24½ x 32"

WOLFGANG LENZ

1925-

The Artist's Collection, Wurtzburg

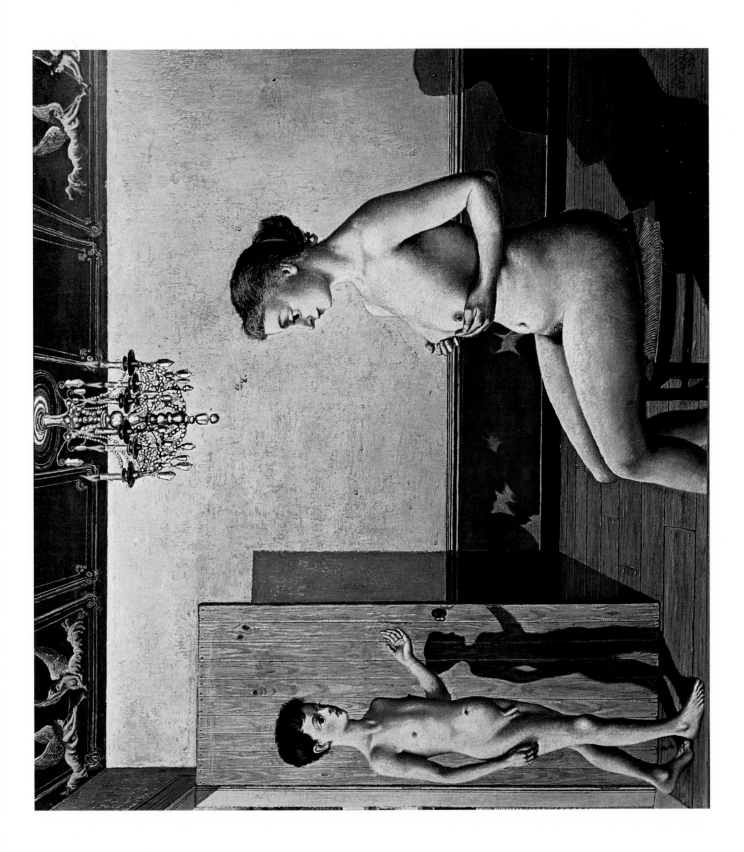

35) The Visit
1939
PAUL DELVAUX
1897-

Private Collection, Paris
Photo—Giraudon

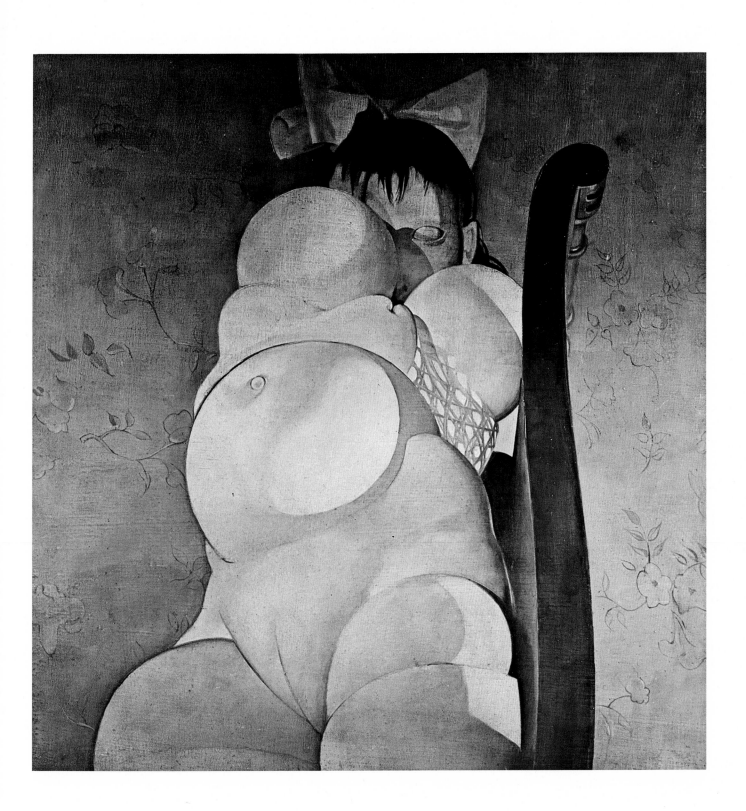

36) Small Painting of a Doll
1941
HANS BELLMER
1902-

Dr. Galy Collection, Paris
Photo—J. Hyde

37) La Chambre
BALTHUS
Hirschhorn Museum, Smithsonian Institute

38) Extasé
1967   28¼ x 30″
PYKE KOCH
1901-

Private Collection, Holland

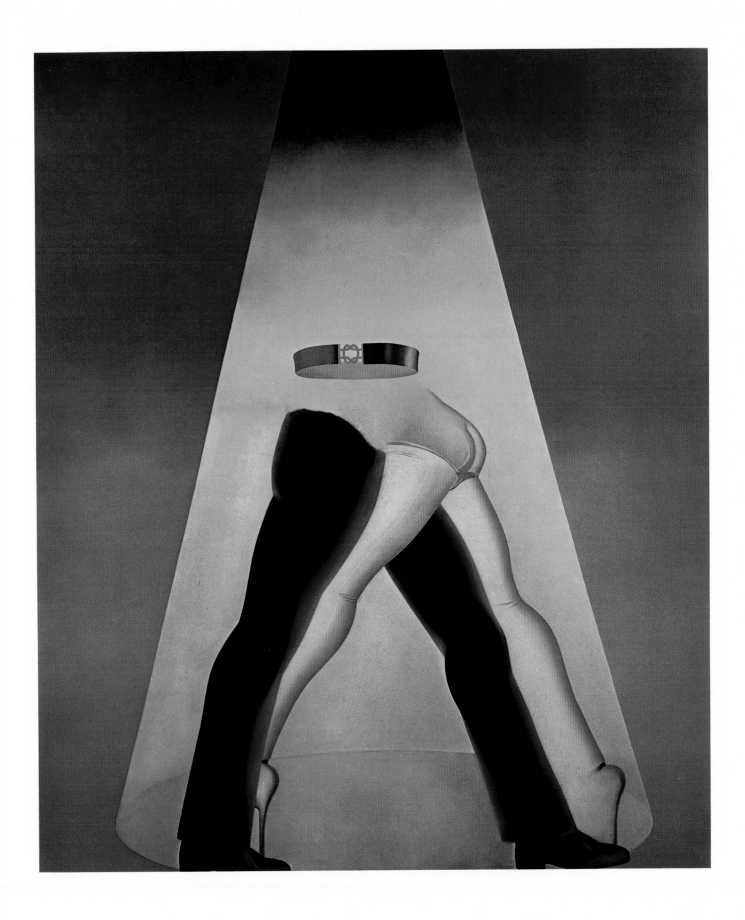

39) Marilyn
1967   72 x 60"
ALLEN JONES
Private Collection, London

40) Silence

1895   21½ x 13¾"

LUCIEN LEVY DHURMER

1865-1953

Private Collection, Paris

Photo—Giraudon